BULLYING
Pocketbook

By Mi‌chele

Phil

Published by:

Teachers' Pocketbooks
Laurel House, Station Approach,
Alresford, Hampshire SO24 9JH, UK
Tel: +44 (0)1962 735573
Fax: +44 (0)1962 733637
E-mail: sales@teacherspocketbooks.co.uk
Website: www.teacherspocketbooks.co.uk

*Teachers' Pocketbooks is an imprint of
Management Pocketbooks Ltd.*

Series Consultant: **Brin Best**.

This edition published 2005.
Reprinted 2007.

ISBN   978 1 903776 70 4

British Library Cataloguing-in-Publication
Data. A catalogue record for this book is
available from the British Library.

Design, typesetting and graphics by Efex Ltd.
Printed in UK.

Contents

Introduction

I remember the first school I taught in, back in the late 1960s. We teachers would gather in the staff room and whisper about the bullying headteacher. Thankfully, we survived and she retired! Bullying is universal, but lots can be done to reduce or even stop it.

This pocketbook has all kinds of ideas, exercises and information that you can suggest or use for assemblies, classes, working with pupils or staff or for an inset day. The ideas come from 35 years of teaching and running the anti-bullying charity Kidscape. They have been gleaned from the thousands of fantastic teachers I've met in my travels.

There is brilliant anti-bullying work going on in schools and one thing we do know about bullying is that teachers can make all the difference. However, there are still a few diehards who think that bullying is a necessary part of life. Together we might convince them otherwise and help prevent a child attempting suicide because he or she is being severely and systematically bullied. We might also prevent a child who is bullying from leading a life of misery and causing others misery.

A tall order for a little book, but I think you'll find it chock-full of practical things you can try. Let me know if you develop something we can share with others for the next edition.

What Do We Know About Bullying?

Defining bullying

Girls in her class called Sally names, but when she complained she was told that it was only a bit of teasing. How often have you heard that? *'It isn't really bullying – it is only name-calling'*. However, any form of deliberate, hurtful behaviour like name-calling IS bullying, if the bully persists knowing the victim is upset by the taunts.

When discussing bullying with pupils (and perhaps staff) it helps if you agree broadly about what bullying is. Professor Dan Olweus, of the University of Bergen, sets down three main features that are always present:

1. There is deliberate aggression.
2. There is an unequal balance of power.
3. The aggression results in pain and distress.

You could either use this definition as it is or see it as a starting point for your own.

> **Bullying is repeated intimidation intentionally carried out by a more powerful person or group in order to cause physical and/or emotional hurt.**

Types of bullying

Asking pupils for examples of bullying often gets a lively discussion going and gives you an insight into what might be happening out there.   Try priming them with a few ideas:

Physical: Pushing, kicking, hitting, pinching and other forms of violence or threats such as, *'I'll be waiting after school to get you if you don't give me your money now'*

Verbal: Name-calling, sarcasm, spreading nasty rumours, cruel teasing

Emotional: Excluding, tormenting, ridiculing, humiliating, threatening gestures

Racist: Using racist taunts, gestures or graffiti

Sexual: Abusive sexual comments, homophobic slurs or gestures

Cyber or online: Texting hurtful comments, setting up hate websites, phoning a mobile to abuse the victim

An exercise

Here's an exercise you could suggest if you are working with a group of colleagues (or pupils) and want to discuss and agree on an acceptable definition of bullying.

Find a partner. Each person tells about an incident of bullying they remember from childhood. It might be something they remember happening to someone else or to themselves. Give the pairs a few minutes to exchange information.

Starting like this brings everyone into the discussion and breaks the ice.

Discussion

Next ask the group to think about the stories and incidents of bullying they are familiar with, and to come up with the key elements that made these incidents 'bullying'.

Note the elements on a flipchart/board/OHP as the group calls them out.

From this you can try to reach agreement on a definition of your own.

HUMILIATING   HURTFUL   PERSISTENT   ABUSIVE

FRIGHTENING   PHYSICAL VIOLENCE   BELITTLING   EXCLUSION

NASTY   SECRET   OSTRACISING

AGGRESSIVE   MENTAL ABUSE   DELIBERATE   SHAMING

Why does bullying happen?

Watching young children grab toys or thump another child over the head because she or he got in the way, makes us wonder if bullying is just part of human nature. Perhaps it is. We all want what we want when we want it, but we learn to modify our behaviour (some of us) and most of us do not go on to bully others.

Bullying happens for a very simple, basic reason: the bully needs a victim and looks for someone to bully. In 99% of cases, the victim has done absolutely nothing to provoke the bully, except to exist. There are a few children who seem to go out of their way to bother people, but we will discuss them in the section on victims.

Why does it continue?
Because no one steps in to stop it and the bully gains more power until it becomes a big problem affecting lots of students and teachers.

How widespread is bullying?

Most studies show that bullying takes place in all schools to some extent. Even if we do our best to tackle it, we all have to deal with it at some time or other.

If someone tells you, *'There has never been any bullying in our school'*, be suspicious. Either they work in a school with two students who are best friends, or they just do not want to know. One mother rang Kidscape to say that her son had been bullied so badly he attempted suicide. The response from the headteacher was that the boy should 'pull himself together because life is tough'. Fortunately most teachers are enlightened and are doing their best to ensure that bullying is eradicated.

It's everywhere

Bullying happens in every type of school and in all classes and cultures. Bullying also occurs in institutions, the work place, religious organisations and agencies of every kind. Little bullies grow up to be big bullies and turn to adult victims after they leave school (or stay in school to bully other teachers and children). Many bullies make life impossible for their own children and families.

Looking at all the studies, it is reasonable to conclude that at any one time about 1 in 7 children are involved in bullying, either as victims or bullies. However, over a whole school career even more children are affected by bullying. I could quote you lots of statistics, but you might get bored; if you are interested, you can find all kinds of research studies on the internet. I think we all agree that bullying is a problem for thousands of children and adults. This book is about what to do to counteract it.

Throughout the book I refer to 'bullies and victims' for purposes of brevity. With children and parents, you might want to say, 'children who are bullied or who bully'.

Bullying matters because...

If you meet resistance to the idea that stopping bullying is important, try a few facts:

- Several young people commit suicide every year because of it
- Over half of the victims of bullying who come to Kidscape's ZAP anti-bullying assertiveness courses (see page 92) have attempted suicide
- Children who are being bullied cannot concentrate on their school work – they can only think about how to get away from their tormentors
- Bullies who are not stopped are four times more likely to end up in prison than people who are not bullies
- Victims and bullies suffer from low self-esteem and lack confidence

There are many more reasons, but suffice to say that bullying has a long-lasting negative effect on everyone involved, not least on teachers who have to deal with it.

Myths about bullying

Knowing how harmful bullying is, these ever-present myths need to be scotched:

> *'Bullying is a normal part of growing-up', or 'Bullying didn't hurt me'*

It doesn't have to be part of growing up. It is possible to create a bully-free environment. The person who says it didn't hurt is probably the bully.

> *'It's character-building'*

Why do children have to be tormented to the edge of despair in order to have their character 'built'? 'Character-destructive' might be a more apt description.

> *'It'll make a man (woman) of him (her)'*

Translation: You become a man/woman by suffering beatings/thefts/taunting in silence. What kind of man or woman and why should a child be forced to suffer agonies in silence?

How bullying thrives

Bullying comes into our lives as teachers all too frequently. We may not be able to stop what is happening to the bully at home or outside our school gates, but within our classrooms bullying thrives when:

- Adults sit back, throw up their hands and say nothing can be done
- Bullying is considered a normal or even essential part of growing up
- Children or young people have too much power over other children
- There is no private way for victims to get help
- Telling is discouraged
- There is no effective anti-bullying policy
- There are no consequences when bullying is discovered
- Victims are blamed for being 'too nice' or 'not tough enough'
- Teachers and staff are afraid of the bully
- Teachers and staff are not backed up when trying to tackle bullying

Teachers getting it right

Headteachers and staff who have managed to stop or drastically reduce bullying have several things in common:

- They have an anti-bullying policy that states, 'this is a telling school' and, 'bullying of any kind is not tolerated'
- They ensure the pupils take in this message through assemblies, classroom work, contracts and posters
- They involve students in writing anti-bullying codes
- They conduct surveys to find out where, when and how bullying is occurring
- They inform parents that bullying will not be tolerated

Go teachers!

Also:

- They ensure there are consequences for bad behaviour and rewards for good behaviour that are clearly stated and known by all and enforced
- They ensure something is done to stop the bullying and to protect victims
- They give pupils access to help privately, so the victims can tell in safety
- They talk about and incorporate anti-bullying strategies in lessons and assemblies
- They train all staff to recognise signs and symptoms of bullying
- They have the proverbial 'eyes in the back of their heads'

Immediate consequences of bullying

When bullying occurs, there are usually immediate
consequences.   Victims may:

- Lose confidence and self-esteem
- Become withdrawn and nervous
- Be unable to concentrate
- Begin to do badly in their
  academic work
- Truant, develop school phobia,
  attempt suicide
- Misbehave at home, causing
  tension within their families

Consequences for bullies

It won't surprise you to know that letting bullies off leads to all kinds of negatives. Other children learn that using aggression/violence is a successful strategy for getting what you want, and as for the bullies, they:

- Realise that they can get away with cruel behaviour, eroding school discipline
- Become divisive as a dominant group – those not in the main group are left out and ignored
- Become more disruptive, eventually testing members of staff to see how far they can push them
- Suffer, as their underlying problems may be masked by aggressive behaviour and go untreated

Long-term consequences of bullying

Kidscape conducted the first retrospective study of 1000 adults who were bullied as children. They said the emotional scars were deep, and that the fear and loneliness they experienced as childhood victims still affected the way they looked at the world.

Adult victims of childhood bullying can suffer from:

- Depression
- Low self-esteem
- Fear of meeting strangers
- Guilt, shame
- Social isolation

- Psychosomatic diseases
- Agoraphobia
- Anxiety/panic attacks
- Exceptional timidity
- Anger

They can also be more susceptible to approaches from cults and other unscrupulous organisations that play on their insecurities.

Stephen, now 34, wrote:
'I learnt not to get angry or cry when they bullied me. I still feel intense pain that is quite difficult to describe. I have felt dirty, degraded and ashamed, and intensely lonely and depressed. I get anxiety attacks. Sometimes, for no reason, I shake and have trouble breathing. So much of my life has been taken over by what they did.'

Jane, aged 29, wrote:
The bullying from girls in my secondary school was so intimidating that I went around with my head down, desperate not to antagonise them. I never knew why they hated me so much. One day, a man on the street invited me to a free lecture about being assertive. I screwed up my courage and went. Everyone was so friendly and welcoming that I felt wanted for the first time. They told me that I was intelligent and exactly the kind of person to take their course. I eventually got sucked into what I now know was a cult. Looking back, I realise that it was my lack of confidence caused by the bullying that made me a perfect target for them. They bullied me into the cult. I am out of it now and getting my life together.'

Long-term consequences for bullies

- Uncontrollable, aggressive behaviour/psychiatric disorders
- Criminal convictions/alcohol abuse
- Abuse of children and partners
- Relationship breakdowns
- Employment problems

One study found that children who were bullies at age 12 were four times more likely than their peers to have criminal convictions for aggression and violence. The long-term outlook for chronic bullies is poor.

Because bullying is so destructive, we must take positive steps to eradicate it. It is not some inevitable natural phenomenon; we can control it. The following chapter has ideas from lots of teachers who have tried – and often succeeded – in tackling this thorny problem. See which of them are useful for you.

Teacher Tips

Staff concerns

Staff members often feel uncertain, annoyed, and even angry about having to get involved in tackling bullying. It is another issue we are expected to deal with on top of all our other duties. This short exercise can help clarify staff worries.

Break into small groups and give each person a copy of the comments on the next page, or make up your own. Each group can choose two or three concerns they think are relevant and discuss them. (The concerns have all been raised in Kidscape workshops, so you can see you're not alone!)

After 10 –15 minutes, come together and discuss your thoughts. You may also want to opt for a few positive solutions so it doesn't turn into just a 'moan session'.

Issues

1. Never mind the children bullying each other, what are we going to do about children bullying the teachers?
2. What about bullies on the staff who bully the kids and other staff members?
3. Bullying takes place going to and from school – is that our problem?
4. What about kids who are bullies and have bullies for parents? What happens when we try to stop their kids being bullies?
5. Won't it seem like we've got a real problem with bullying if we start to bring it out in the open? Will we get a reputation as a 'bully school'?
6. This is just one more issue that is in fashion. We should just ignore it and get on with teaching. We've got more than enough to do already.

It's amazing how many legitimate concerns emerge once you start discussing bullying.

What is our role?

Adults affect bullying in three ways:

1. We **permit** it by our lack of concern for victims and by not tackling incidents.
2. We **promote** it by our attitudes and by allowing bullies to get away with it.
3. We **prevent** it by taking action and by challenging bullying whenever it takes place.

Permitting

Bullying is **permitted** by teachers when:

- Victims are ignored or blamed
- We do not listen to what children tell us
- Victims who tell are told to sort it out themselves
- Victims are too scared to tell
- We encourage retaliation
- There are no effective policies or procedures for dealing with bullying
- Bullies know nothing will happen and gain power

Promoting

Bullying is **promoted** by teachers when:

- We are dismissive of what children tell us
- We are aggressive and sarcastic role models
- We humiliate children in front of their peers
- We pick on individuals or roll our eyes when they approach us
- We are impatient with the less able or irritating children
- We are unapproachable and insensitive
- We do not set limits or consequences to bad behaviour
- Classroom management is poor

Preventing

Bullying is **prevented** by teachers when:

- We listen to children and encourage them to tell about bullying
- We are fair
- Differences between individuals are celebrated
- We raise children's self-esteem
- We are assertive, not aggressive, role models
- Anti-bullying policies and procedures are devised and implemented
- We act immediately to stop and condemn bullying, fighting or cruelty
- We make it clear to pupils that there will be consequences for bullying
- We keep records of incidents
- We do not blame victims for being bullied
- We encourage and reward good behaviour

Attitudes

If we are serious about wanting to tackle bullying in our schools, we have to examine our own attitudes first. When staff display bullying behaviour, no matter how good our school's anti-bullying policy is, pupils will get the message that bullying is acceptable.

Professor Dan Olweus (see page 6) concludes:

> *'The attitudes, routines, and behaviours of the school personnel, particularly those of the teachers, are **decisive factors** in preventing and controlling bullying activities, as well as in redirecting such behaviours into more socially acceptable channels.'*

I met and worked with Dan in Norway, where he has managed almost to eradicate bullying. I was impressed by how much of what he said turned out to be true.

The ball of string exercise

This is a simple and fun exercise that shows what happens if a school or institution does not have an effective anti-bullying policy.

One colleague acts as the 'victim'. Everyone else chooses a role from the list on the next page or takes another role of their choice. The 'victim' is given a ball of string that represents 'bullying'. The 'victim' **holds** one end of the string and throws the ball to a participant playing a role (mother, for example). This represents telling about the bullying and asking for help.

The 'mother', keeping hold of the string, then throws the ball to another colleague and so on until everyone has caught the ball, held on to a bit and thrown it on. At the end, the room should look like a cat's cradle with everyone linked by a tangled muddle of string.

This is what can happen when there is no effective procedure for dealing with bullying. Everyone gets dragged into the problem.

The ball of string exercise

Try the exercise again, except this time **cut** the string when the 'role' person deals with the bullying instead of passing it on.

Result: no tangle and bullying stopped.

It is fun to do this on Friday afternoon with light refreshments!

Roles

BULLY

FRIEND

RELIGIOUS LEADER

CLASS TEACHER

YEAR HEAD

HEADTEACHER

MOTHER

FATHER

OTHER RELATIVE

PARENT GOVERNOR

SCHOOL NURSE

NEIGHBOUR

CHAIR OF GOVERNORS

SCHOOL COUNSELLOR

POLICE OFFICER

MEALS SUPERVISOR

SCHOOL CARETAKER

BUS DRIVER

EDUCATIONAL PSYCHOLOGIST

LOCAL COUNCILLOR

EDUCATION WELFARE OFFICER

MP

Schools designed for bullies

Old buildings with poky rooms and long, dark corridors provide plenty of places where bullies can corner their victims. Outside buildings like bike-sheds are a bully paradise. Although we cannot rebuild our schools, we can ensure that supervision is adequate and we can encourage victims to tell where and when they were bullied in order to pin down likely trouble spots or times.

In one school bullying was rife at break-times so the headteacher moved his office to a room overlooking the playground. Bullying diminished rapidly once the bullies realised their **every move was monitored** by a glance out of the window.

Governors in another school approved the use of a camera that was trained on the playground during breaks. Just knowing that they might be **captured on film** stopped the bullying behaviour almost overnight. **Use a fake camera if your budget is tight**.

Supervision

Adequate supervision of students is very important. Playground supervisors and catering staff should be involved in the anti-bullying policy from the beginning; they are well placed to see if bullying continues and to identify both bullies and victims.

Staff attitudes, the physical layout of the school and the adequacy of supervision arrangements are all important when devising anti-bullying strategies.

Other factors that can promote bullying are:

- Low staff morale
- High teacher turnover
- Unclear standards of behaviour
- Inconsistent methods of discipline
- Remote and unapproachable staff

Take a look at the 'perfect school for bullies' on the next page. Or you might want to ask your pupils to design one; it can be a real eye opener to what is happening.

A perfect school for bullies

The list opposite is not meant to be exhaustive – everyone will have something to add! It was compiled by Peter Smith and Peter Stephenson, teachers and psychologists who have extensively researched bullying in the UK. One teacher said the list 'perfectly described' his school.

- Unsupervised toilets/bike-sheds
- No space for 'quiet' activities
- Bare, empty, unsupervised playground
- Not enough equipment in gyms and labs
- Areas where staff never go
- Whole school queueing at once for meals
- Old buildings with dark, secluded corners
- Staff never around – always in staffroom
- Staff too busy to notice incidents
- Unsupervised meal queues
- Narrow, dark corridors
- Crowded locker rooms
- Everyone arriving and leaving at once
- Long changeovers between lessons
- Teachers being late/leaving class early
- Chaotic classrooms
- Teachers who point/shout/poke
- Teachers who use sarcasm as a weapon
- No support for pupils with special needs
- No support for new pupils
- Staff who bully
- Reporting bullying seen as 'telling tales'
- No clear procedures for dealing with bullying
- General lack of supervision and discipline

Immediate action

Successful intervention is at the heart of an effective whole school anti-bullying strategy. Reporting incidents is also vital: all students must understand that if they bully, they will be reported and all reports will be followed up.

It is important to deal with the immediate fall-out from the bullying incident as quickly as possible, given all the other constraints on staff time. Delay can be interpreted as hesitation on the part of the staff and this can undermine the positive message that bullying will not be tolerated.

You should try to keep the investigation simple and not get too bogged down in details. You will need to listen to both sides of the story or you may miss the problems that each side has or, worse, be seen as refusing to be impartial.

Just and only

'Just' and 'only' are key words often used by bullies to defend their behaviour. They are used to diminish the seriousness of whatever has happened.

Examples:
'I **only** pushed her'
'I **just** hit him once'
'We were **only** teasing'

From the victims' viewpoint, they were pushed, or hit – 'only' and 'just' are irrelevant.

Try banning the words 'only' and 'just' from all explanations. So, change 'I only pushed her'; 'I just kicked her once', to 'I pushed her'; 'I kicked her once.'

Game, joke, accident

Teachers are often told, by way of excuse, *'It was a game'*, or *'It was a joke'*, or *'It was an accident'*. So, try asking these questions to clarify what you are told:

'It was a game'.
Did everyone join in? Was anybody left out? Did they want to be left out? If it really was a game, then everyone should have been happy to play and those not playing would have chosen not to join in.

'It was a joke'.
Was everyone laughing? Did everyone find it funny? If it really was a joke, as alleged, then everyone should be amused.

'It was an accident'.
Has someone gone to fetch help? Has anyone apologised? Is anyone comforting the person who has been hurt? This is what happens after a real accident. If it's not happening, then whatever happened was not 'an accident'.

No excuses

Sometimes excuses can be bizarre: one mother, when told her daughter had been fighting other girls, said, *'I'm sure she hit them in a nice way.'*

Borrowing is often used as a way to excuse bullying. Try banning it. This eliminates the bully claiming the disputed item was 'borrowed'. One school makes children borrow only from staff and keeps records.

The object of not accepting these lame excuses is to get the bullies to own up to what they have done and not to rationalise away the pain they have caused others. Otherwise the bullies' behaviour will not change and the excuses will go on and on.

Action plan

The steps on this page and the next are given as a general guide. You will want to include your own particular requirements.

- If you witness bullying, the first step is obviously to stop it and remove the bully, perhaps to a 'time-out' area where they can go and cool off
- Reassure victims that they will be protected. If pupils come forward to tell you about bullying, praise them for telling
- If the victim is hurt, seek medical attention and/or ring parents
- If there are bruises or cuts, it might be useful to take pictures so that later denials of harm can be dealt with quickly
- Ask the bully to think of ways to atone for his/her actions – insist on compensation for items lost, damaged or stolen, the return of items 'borrowed' or stolen, and the repayment of money stolen

Action plan

The bully should then apologise to the victim. The bully may not feel genuine remorse; nevertheless, accept even the most grudging apology. Work towards teaching *how to apologise*. We want to teach that hurting people is wrong and that when you hurt someone you acknowledge this to yourself and to the person you have hurt. Saying sorry is the first step towards recognising that bullying behaviour is wrong.

Alternatively, if the bullying involves squabbling or minor incidents between generally well-motivated children, sort the situation out by sitting down and getting them to talk about what happened and why. A round discussion gives everyone a chance to air any grievances and to resolve minor incidents.

Consequences

You may need to help children who bully to understand that:

- Aggressive, violent, or cruel behaviour is unacceptable and if they act in this way they will face consequences

- If assault or theft is involved, it may be necessary to contact police. (The parents of the victim will need to be consulted – some will not press charges and will not be happy if the police are called)

You may want to try **additional consequences**, such as:

- Withdrawal of school journey privileges
- Filling in a report, sending a letter home and/or holding a meeting with parents
- Helping the bully discuss his/her actions with a peer mentor

More ideas for consequences

Teachers say these ideas work at least sometimes:

- Assigning a senior pupil to monitor/befriend the bully
- Having the bully assist a member of staff with special tasks at break times
- Keeping bullies in during breaks or have them eat alone
- Having the bully do his/her work in a room alone for a day/a week
- If the bully is bothering pupils on the way home from school, keeping the bully behind to allow the other children to go home unmolested
- Photographing the bully's actions so he/she can't say, '*I didn't do it*'
- Assigning the bully to extra duties: sorting and stacking books in the library, checking cloakrooms at the end of the day (with praise for doing well)

One school that had an epidemic of pupils kicking each other, decided that a child caught kicking would have his/her shoes removed for the day and wear slippers instead. They had permission from parents.

Telling off!

I am indebted to many teachers like Eric Jones, who has had years of experience as a Deputy Head and classroom teacher and who calls it as he sees it. He says not to forget that the *good old fashioned telling-off, done formally, without interruption, and then put on record* can be very effective. He warns not to be sarcastic, vengeful or personally insulting, but to state facts about unacceptable behaviour and consequences to actions. *It should point towards the future, hoping for something better, expecting something better* and then *the incident put behind us with the culprit being given a chance to prove him/herself or otherwise*.

Some of us may be too worried about false accusations to give this a try, but please let me know your best 'Teacher Tips': michele@kidscape.org.uk In the meantime, delve into the ideas in the next chapter to create that bully-free school.

Creating a Bully-free School

Start with parents

Having absorbed a few tips from other teachers, try the practical step-by-step ways in this chapter to engage parents/carers, survey pupils, set up contracts and review your anti-bullying policy.

The start of the school year is the ideal time to talk with parents about possible problems before they actually arise, so that no one feels defensive. In the first meeting, in the midst of trumpeting your fantastic lunchroom, staff and students, point out that children make mistakes, do nasty things, and that you will need the parents' help all along the way. Gain their trust before any bullying begins.

It is also a good idea to write to parents to let them know about your anti-bullying policy. In the past, the reputation of some schools has suffered as parents have mistakenly assumed that because the school was tackling bullying, it must have a major bullying problem. This is an unfortunate misconception, so a letter setting out the school's anti-bullying policy will clarify the situation, reassure parents and prevent the switchboard lighting up with 100 telephone calls! The most common complaint on the Kidscape helpline is that schools don't tell parents about their anti-bullying policy or strategies.

Contact with home

If you have to contact parents or carers about their child being a bully (always difficult and usually denied vehemently) or a victim, try asking if anything has happened lately:

- Has anything happened which could explain the bullying?
- What do they think is happening at school?
- Is the child bullying or being bullied by anyone at home?
- Did they know, and how long have they known, about the bullying?
- Have they talked to their child about his/her concerns and worries?
- Have they been approached by the bully's/victim's family? Outcome?
- Has anything like this happened before? How was it resolved?
- Have the parents any ideas for working with you to sort out the problem?

Assure the parents that you will deal with the situation and keep them informed. Give them the advice on the next two pages and they will feel you are trying to help.

Advice for parents of children who are being bullied

- Don't ignore the problem – talk to the teachers and work together
- Encourage your child to talk to you about his/her feelings
- Try not to over-react – it might frighten your child into silence
- Ask your child if he/she has any suggestions that would help
- Find out if your child feels safe and protected
- Take any threats of suicide or other desperate pleas seriously and seek help – children sometimes go to extremes if they are miserable
- Help your child develop strategies for dealing with and reporting bullying – Kidscape has advice on www.kidscape.org.uk
- Praise your child, tell him/her how much you love and support them
- Try to sort out the bullying at the start, as constructively as possible, with the school
- Encourage your child to develop new interests which might lead to a supportive group of friends – in school and out of school

Advice for parents of children who are bullying

- Calmly ask your child if he/she can explain what has happened and why
- Find out if there are ways you can work together to stop his/her behaviour
- Explain that the bullying must stop – there is no compromise on this
- Explain how frightening the bullying is for the victim and encourage empathy
- Criticise the bullying behaviour, but don't reject your child or label him/her as a 'bully' ('*What you did was wrong*' not '*You're a terrible person or a bully*')
- Look for good behaviour from your child and praise it
- Tell your child you know he/she can change bullying behaviour and that your child is NOT really a bully. Be confident that your child will change
- Help your child to develop new interests and/or friends away from bullies
- Spend as much time with your child as you can, especially listening to his/her concerns. Sometimes children bully as a way of getting attention
- Make it clear that you do not accept bullying behaviour and there will be consequences such as loss of privileges if the bullying does not stop

Student councils

Having gained the support of parents, now try setting up effective ways to work with pupils.

One way that has worked in many schools is enlisting the support of the student council. Part of its remit can be to deal with positive ways to tackle bullying. Pupils usually know much more about the bullying situation in a school than the adults, which is hardly surprising. Using their good will and expertise can dramatically cut down the time you have to spend dealing with incidents.

The council can set the tone and help devise, distribute and collate questionnaires about bullying (see the following pages). It can suggest ways to keep children safe and even possible consequences for bullying behaviour. This does not imply draconian solutions. School councils have opted for a time-out place for the bully to cool off, suggested ways the bully could be more effective in making friends, made sure that victims had a 'buddy' or that new pupils were given mentors.

'Bullying' questionnaire

Work with the student council to write and oversee a questionnaire/survey to find out:

- If bullying is taking place
- If pupils are interested or concerned
- Where it is happening
- When it is happening
- Patterns of bullying
- What groups are involved in bullying

Ensure the format allows answers to be anonymous (see following pages).

How to use the questionnaire

It could be a small group of staff volunteers who work with the pupils to devise a questionnaire. Some schools also include parents in this process, which helps to eliminate any future misunderstandings. Alternatively, you can use or adapt the following questionnaires to save time and your sanity.

Give copies to every pupil. It is best if the students fill out their questionnaires anonymously – they will more likely answer honestly. Pupils may be worried that their handwriting will be recognised. To overcome this, the questionnaire could have tick boxes; the format will obviously depend upon the age and abilities of children. Some children may need help to fill in the answers, so anonymity may not be possible.

When the findings are summarised, discuss and distribute them to the whole staff, including meals and playground supervisors, and the pupils.

Sample questionnaire for young children

Ask the children to fill in the blanks with drawings or with happy or sad faces or words. You will obviously have to leave more space for drawing than I can include here.

Who makes you happy?

Does anyone make you unhappy?

Draw a happy or a sad face to show if you are happy or unhappy in these places:

 Playground   Classroom

 Toilets   Lunchroom

 Coming to school   Going home from school

Young person questionnaire

a) Have you ever been bullied in this school? ☑ yes ☐ no.

b) When? ☐ now ☑ sometime this year ☐ in the past.

c) Did/do you consider the bullying ☐ not bad ☐ worrying ☑ terrible?

d) Was it so bad that you didn't want to go to school? ☐ yes ☐ no.

e) Did the bullying ☐ have no effect ☐ some bad effect ☐ terrible effect ☐ make you want to change schools?

f) Is the bullying still happening? ☐ yes ☐ no.

g) If the bullying is still happening, where is it occurring? ☐ classroom ☐ halls ☐ during sports ☐ toilet ☐ after school ☐ lunchroom ☐ library ☐ activities ☐ breaktime ☐ everywhere.

h) How often is the bullying happening? ☐ seldom ☐ once a day ☐ several times a day ☐ once a week ☐ once a month ☐ all the time.

i) Is the bullying ☐ physical ☐ verbal ☐ racial ☐ homophobic ☐ sexual ☐ emotional (being ignored etc) ☐ threat ☐ taking possessions ☐ text ☐ email ☐ mobile ☐ website?

j) Do you know anyone who is being bullied, but has not told? ☐ yes ☐ no.

k) Are you a ☐ girl ☐ boy?

l) Is the bully (or bullies) ☐ girl ☐ boy ☐ both ☐ a gang ☐ teacher ☐ other member of staff ☐ other?

m) If you were or are being bullied, have you ever told anyone? ☐ yes ☐ no.

n) Did the bullying stop when you told? ☐ yes ☐ no.

o) Did the bullying become worse because you told? ☐ yes ☐ no.

p) Have you ever bullied anyone? ☐ yes ☐ no.

q) Are you bullying someone in this school now? ☐ yes ☐ no.

r) What should be done about the problem of bullying? (Optional)

School contracts

A carefully devised contract is a good way of ensuring that everybody knows what they can and cannot do. Nobody can say, *'I didn't know it wasn't allowed'*. If bullying takes place, victims know that they can tell and bullies know that they will not be able to depend on the silence of victims or witnesses for protection.

Contracts are not just imposed arbitrarily upon the student body. They are discussed and amended, and the final version is the result of agreement and compromise.

Why a school contract?

So what are the advantages of a school contract?

- Everybody knows what is acceptable and expected of them
- They provide clear simple guidelines
- They eliminate *'I didn't know it wasn't allowed'* excuse
- Students from different racial and cultural backgrounds are protected
- Sexual harassment and homophobia are outlawed
- They teach pupils how to behave as responsible members of the school
- They involve pupils so that they 'own' it and it reflects their concern

Using the contract

If contracts are printed on coloured paper they are easily visible and retrievable. You may also wish to put a notation on the contract of the year or term it covers. There are a number of ways of using contracts.

- The final version of the contract can be distributed to every pupil
- Each pupil and their parents can be asked to sign a copy to be kept in the pupil's file
- Copies can be displayed in classrooms, corridors and main hall
- A copy of the contract can be included in the parents' handbook, or a copy can be sent home
- It can be read to each class at the beginning of term and to each new pupil

Bullying is obviously not the only issue on the agenda: schedules, rosters, lunch arrangements, anti-racism, equal opportunities, homework policies and all sorts of other things may also need to be displayed. Displaying *only* the anti-bullying policy on the school contract may lead visitors to conclude that bullying is rife! Include a variety of issues in the contract, all of which apply to most schools, such as taking responsibility in the school, littering, vandalism, acceptance of others, etc.

Sample contract designed by 11 year olds

CONTRACT

1. We will not tolerate bullying or harassing of any kind.

2. We will be accepting of all races, religions, cultures and disabilities.

3. If we see anyone being bullied, we will either try to stop it or go for help.

4. We will not allow bullying or harassing going to or from school, whether walking, on the school bus or on public transport.

5. We will allow a quiet area at break for those who do not want to play games.

6. We will use our 'time out' room if we feel angry or under pressure or just need time to calm down or work out what is wrong.

7. We will not litter or draw on school property.

8. We will be kind to others, even if they are not our friends and we will make new students feel welcome.

9. On school journeys we will act in a way which brings credit to our school.

10. We will be honest about anything we have done.

11. We will have a discussion group once a week in class to talk about problems.

12. We will support the student council and be nice to teachers. (Good idea!)

Sample contract designed by teachers

C O N T R A C T

1. We will behave sensibly and with consideration for others when in school.

2. We will take turns in a queue.

3. We will not interfere with other people's property or bring valuables to school.

4. We will not pick on other students and will respect other people's opinions.

5. We will report any bullying or fighting incidents to a member of staff.

6. Staff and students will talk politely and give each other a fair hearing.

7. We should have a quiet, supervised area to go to away from others.

8. We will be willing to help other students if necessary.

9. Staff will supervise 'trouble spots'.

10. We will not join in fights or disturbances but will report them to staff.

11. We will make the playground a fun place to be, with enough things to do.

12. We will look after new students.

Producing an anti-bullying policy

Every school is required by law to have an anti-bullying policy. It may seem like just one more thing to do, but it does make dealing with bullying easier in the long run. When parents, staff and pupils know the policy and what will happen, it often cuts down the hassle when bullying rears its ugly head. You probably already have a policy, but if not, here are some suggestions for starting the ball rolling. You can:

1. Break into small groups to work on one particular phase of the policy.
2. Break into small groups and each come up with a complete policy.
3. Give each group a copy of the Kidscape anti-bullying policy and adapt it.
4. Look at your own anti-bullying policy and accept or revise it.
5. Consider adding a help section with local and national numbers.

Kidscape anti-bullying policy

The Kidscape anti-bullying policy, which has evolved from years of working with schools, appears here and on the next two pages. You can adapt it to your own needs or write your own.

'We are committed to providing a caring, friendly and safe environment for our pupils. Bullying of any kind is unacceptable. If bullying does occur, all pupils should be able to tell and know that incidents will be dealt with promptly and effectively. We are a TELLING school – anyone who knows that bullying is happening is expected to tell.'

What is bullying?
Bullying is the use of aggression with the <u>deliberate</u> intention of hurting another person:

Physical:	Pushing, kicking, hitting, pinching and other forms of violence or threats
Verbal:	Name-calling, sarcasm, spreading nasty rumours
Emotional:	Excluding, tormenting, ridiculing, humiliating, threatening gestures
Racist:	Using racist taunts, gestures or graffiti
Sexual:	Unwanted contact, abusive sexual comments, homophobic slurs
Cyber/online:	Texting or phoning threats, setting up hate websites, chat room misuse

Kidscape anti-bullying policy

Objectives
- All staff, governors, pupils and parents know school anti-bullying policy
- Bullying will not be tolerated and will be dealt with effectively
- Clear procedures for reporting bullying are understood and followed

Procedures and consequences
1. Report bullying incidents to staff.
2. Incidents will be recorded by staff, unless minor and sorted out.
3. Parents should be informed if serious case and asked to discuss the problem.
4. If necessary and appropriate, police will be consulted.
5. Bullying behaviour and threats must be investigated and immediately stopped.
6. An attempt will be made to help bullies change their behaviour.
7. Bullies will apologise and other appropriate consequences may take place.
8. In serious cases, suspension or exclusion will be considered.
9. Whenever possible, the pupils will be reconciled.

Kidscape anti-bullying policy

Signs and symptoms

Pupils may indicate by signs or behaviour that they are being bullied.   They may:

- Be frightened of walking to or from school or be unwilling to go to school
- Begin to do poorly in school work
- Become withdrawn, start stammering, stop eating
- Regularly have books or clothes destroyed/possessions 'go missing'
- Become distressed, stop eating, cry easily, have nightmares
- Become disruptive or aggressive
- Start stealing money (to pay bully)
- Be frightened to tell or nervous of messages received on mobile or internet
- Attempt suicide or run away

You can add local and national helplines or advice centres or specific consequences to your policy to round it off.   Some schools give a copy to all parents, pupils and staff. Some put it in the school handbook.

Once you have all these things in place, you can get the pupils actively involved in the discussions and activities in the following chapter.

Awareness-raising
for Pupils

Telling

Getting pupils to talk about and understand bullying is crucial, so here are a few discussion topics and ideas for pupil involvement. There are more in the 'Suggestions for Everyone' section later.

Ask pupils to discuss when it is right to tell about incidents of bullying.

- Do they think of telling as sneaking, grassing, telling tales?
- Is it right to tell if telling will help another person out of trouble or other difficulties like bullying?
- Is it right to tell if telling means getting other people into trouble?
- Is it right to tell to protect yourself?
- When would it be wrong to tell?

The answers are along the lines that it is never wrong to tell if someone is being bullied or hurt. Not telling means you are colluding with the bullies.

Witnessing bullying

Ask pupils to think about those involved in bullying incidents.

- What about bullies? How do you think they feel?
- What about victims? How do you think they feel?
- What about those who see what is going on but do nothing to stop it?
- If people walk past and do nothing, are they to blame?
- Should you get into trouble if you don't help?
- What could you do to help the victims?

It is important that students understand that, where bullying is concerned, there is no such thing as an 'innocent bystander'. If someone sees what is going on and does nothing to stop it, or does not tell or get help, then that person is part of the bullying.

Bully gangs

Ask pupils to discuss bully gangs.

- Why do you think pupils bully in a gang?
- Are those in a bully gang all equally to blame?
- What could you do if you had become involved in a gang and you wanted out but were frightened?
- What could you do if you knew someone was being bullied by a gang?

Talk about breaking the power of the gang. This usually means all the 'hanger-on' kids agreeing not to follow the bully gang leader, thus breaking his/her power.

TV, films and books

Ask pupils to think of bullying situations they have seen in films or TV programmes (Soaps!) or read about in books. *Harry Potter* and *Lord of the Flies* come to mind.

Ask them to describe briefly what happened.

- Were the scenes scary to see or read about?
- Did they empathise most with the victim or the bully?
- Why did the bully act the way he or she did?
- Could the victim get help to stop the bullying?
- Does bullying only happen in schools?
- How do they spot that bullying is going on?

Hold an anti-bullying week

Schools have successfully organized anti-bullying weeks.
Ideas for the week:

- Produce a magazine or newsletter
- Design posters
- Show videos/DVDs
- Stage an assembly with readings of stories and poems written by students
- Write a play about bullying and perform it to parents
- Write a short story or poem from a victim's viewpoint
- Write a short story or poem from a bully's viewpoint

Give prizes for the best ideas. Invite local media to cover it.

Produce an anti-bullying magazine

Pupils from different year groups could meet once a week (perhaps at lunchtime with a parent volunteer) to work on an anti-bullying magazine. They could

- Write stories about bullies and victims
- Make up quizzes, puzzles
- Write poems, rap songs
- Draw pictures

During the anti-bullying week sell the magazine to everyone connected with the school. (Or put an anti-bullying page in the school magazine with problems, poems and puzzles.)

Poster competition

Encourage all pupils to take part in an anti-bullying poster design competition. Display the posters during the anti-bullying week. Use the money raised by selling the anti-bullying magazine to fund prizes for the best poster designs. Convince a local business or local printer to print the best design as the school anti-bullying poster. Display it in every classroom and in the corridors and get it published in the local paper.

Rip Rip: the torment of a child

If you want to help primary and middle school pupils understand how verbal bullying can affect people, try this exercise.   Some teachers ask older pupils to do the exercise with younger pupils as an anti-bullying project.

Draw the outline of a child and photocopy it for each pupil. Ask them to rip their cut-out a little bit every time they think the figure is hurt by something in the story you are going to read out:

Rip Rip
I can't wait to get to school. I know it's going to be fun. Oh, look, here come some other kids. They go to my school. They're waiting for the school bus.

What are they looking at? Me? They seem to be sniggering and pointing at me. Why? I didn't do anything to them. What are they saying? Stupid? **Rip Rip**

Here come some other children. Maybe they will stop those kids making fun of me. Oh, they're looking away and pretending not to hear. I wish they would help. **Rip Rip**

Rip Rip: the torment of a child

I'll just look at the ground and keep to myself. I'm too ashamed to meet anyone's eyes. The bus driver is yelling at me to hurry up. They're laughing. **Rip Rip**

In Maths class I was daydreaming and the teacher drew a red line through my work. The kids giggled. **Rip Rip**

In the playground they made fun of me. The supervisor thought we were all having fun. I wanted to tell her. But they told me to shut up or 'you'll get worse'. **Rip Rip**

At lunch they told no one to sit with me. I never did anything to them – why are they doing this to me? **Rip Rip**

I was washing my hands in the toilets when they came in. 'Why are you washing your hands? You need to wash your whole body.' Do I? **Rip Rip**

Rip Rip: the torment of a child

In science class we studied primates. There were pictures of monkeys. When I left the class, some of them were standing outside and they started making monkey noises and gestures as I walked by. It was the last straw. I screamed at them, tears running down my face, 'WHY ARE YOU DOING THIS TO ME? WHAT HAVE I DONE TO YOU?' **Rip Rip**

The teacher heard me screaming. They said I'd been bothering them all day. I got into trouble. I feel like I'm in shreds. **Rip Rip Rip**

The figures will now be in shreds. Discuss how it feels to be bullied and what could have happened differently at each stage of the day. How could they have helped?

Dear bully

Ask your pupils to write a letter to a bully of their choice or, for younger pupils, to the bullies in the previous Rip Rip story to try to explain to the bully how to change his or her behaviour. You can also use this to teach them how to write a real letter, not an email. OK , go ahead and make it an email, if it is easier! It's the thought that counts.

This will lead them and you into the next chapter, which tries to shed some light on why children bully and why some children could be sending out 'victim' signals.

What Do We Know About Bullying?

 Teacher Tips

 Creating a Bully-free School

 Awareness-raising for Pupils

 Understanding Bullies and Victims

 Helping the Bullied and the Bullies

 Suggestions for Everyone

Understanding Bullies and Victims

Children who bully

Children who bully can be high-spirited, active and energetic. They may be easily bored or envious and/or insecure. They may have a learning disability which makes them angry and frustrated (though this may have the opposite effect and make them a target for bullies rather than a bully). They may be angry or down-trodden from what they have suffered. Here are some possible characteristics of children who bully:

1. Neglected child
If a child is neglected or punished excessively at home, they may develop a very negative self-image. They may become frustrated, anxious and insecure. They start to bully others in order to gain respect and to prove that they are worthy of notice.

Children who bully

2. From an aggressive family
Families may be aggressive or quick-tempered with lots of loud arguments and shouting. When this is the child's first behaviour model, they will tend to reproduce the same type of aggressive behaviour.

If the parents are bullies, they are likely to defend or promote aggressiveness in their children. This is especially true of some macho-type parents. In one case, a boy set another's clothes on fire. When the father of the bully was told, he was extremely aggressive and refused to accept his child was in any way responsible for what he had done to the victim: *'It's his own fault if he got set on fire'*.

3. From an 'anything goes' family
The child may be given a great deal of licence at home and so have trouble recognising what is acceptable when they are with other people. They may react badly to discipline. They may be spoilt and used to being the centre of attention at home.

Children who bully

4. Occasional bullies

Occasional bullies can be charming, but resort to bullying when it suits. Their bullying behaviour is not consistent and is often precipitated by a crisis or by the bully 'having a bad day'. They

- Are suddenly aggressive to peers, parents, teachers and siblings
- Act impulsively and regret it later
- Don't learn from their mistakes
- May be physically strong
- May be articulate and manipulative
- May display other anti-social behaviours, such as throwing tantrums or yelling
- May, on the whole, have good self-esteem
- May be spoilt rotten at home

These children need firm, clear guidelines and established consequences to actions. We also have to try to teach them to empathise with other children. Their parents are usually cooperative.

Children who bully

5. Chronic bullies

This is the most worrying type of bullying behaviour. These children go from incident to incident, school to school, and may eventually end up being excluded from mainstream education. They attack weakness in others, giving themselves an illusion of power and accomplishment. They

- Act aggressively much of the time and are rarely able to control themselves
- Have a positive attitude towards violence and are disruptive and manipulative
- Refuse to take responsibility for their actions
- Have absolutely no empathy with victims
- Feel inadequate, insecure and humiliated
- Are bullied or severely and inconsistently punished or abused by parents
- Are not allowed to show positive feelings
- Feel they are different or stupid and lack acceptable social skills

Without intensive help, this kind of bully is more likely to go on to commit crimes and cause great distress to others throughout their lives. Their parents may be difficult, but you already know that.

Bullies' reactions

One way of identifying bullies is by the way they react when they cause others pain. A normal reaction is to admit the wrong, even if only to oneself. Usually people feel remorse and apologise. Bullies, however, have difficulty in admitting that they have done anything wrong. They suppress guilt and, because they do not feel remorse, have no hesitation in repeating the hurtful action.

Chronic bully's reaction to hurting someone:
- Justify hurting them to oneself
- Suppress guilt, which often becomes bad mood
- Avoid atonement

Normal reaction to hurting someone:
- Admit wrongdoing, at least to oneself
- Feel guilty
- Atone – do something to make-up

Recognising victims

Children become victims of bullying for many reasons, but the main cause is that bullies need victims and they will find a reason to bully. Bullying is rarely the fault of the victim. Most victims are gentle, intelligent children from caring families and cannot understand why they have been singled out. The sad fact is that the bullies will bully until they find someone they can hurt.

Some children are **chronic victims**. They seem always to end up being bullied – at home, in school, in activities, in organisations such as scouts or guides or youth groups, etc. It is difficult to tell if they feel bad about themselves *because* they have been bullied, ie the bullying created a 'victim' mentality, or if they had other problems which led to them being singled out for bullying.

Chronic victims

Children who are chronic victims often

- Feel bad about themselves and have low self-esteem
- Find that bullying is reassuring – it confirms their low opinion of themselves
- Get upset if told they are good – it doesn't fit into their self-image
- Destroy their own good work
- Say no one likes them
- Are over-sensitive and/or intense
- Lack humour
- Are slow to settle into new situations
- Are jumpy and wary of people

These are children who seem to be bullied wherever they go. Changing schools in order to avoid a persistent bully often has little effect because they are quickly 'identified' as victims by their new classmates. The bullying then begins all over again.

'Different' victims

Bullies will seize on any excuse to get at a victim and will use 'difference' as an excuse to target them. It may be children from a different racial, cultural or religious background. They may wear glasses, or a hearing aid, have asthma, be talented athletes, be gay or lesbian, or be academically gifted or quite good-looking. Whatever the 'difference', it is enough to make them stand out from their peers.

The irony is that there are millions of people with such 'differences' who are not bullied. This may be because adults have prepared children to value differences or because the children never encountered a determined bully. But bullying often depends upon the response of the child when first bullied. Articulate, confident children may easily deflect attempts to bully them and the bully seeks easier targets. Less confident children may be intimidated if the bullying persists, and may eventually display some of the characteristics, like low self-esteem and timidity, associated with chronic victims.

Accidental victims

Accidental victims are those who have not been especially targeted by the bully, but who happen to be in the wrong place at the wrong time. They may be drawn into a bullying incident in which another child is the primary target. They may be trapped by bullies looking for someone to pick on. The majority of the victims who contact Kidscape fall into this category. They aren't even 'different' in a way that stands out – they are just nice kids.

The message for any children who are bullied is that **no one deserves to be bullied** and **the fault lies with the bully, not with them**.

The next chapter outlines some methods to help both bullies and victims. Many of the exercises which follow could benefit all pupils (and probably a few staff as well!). The only difficulty is finding the time in a busy schedule.

Helping the Bullied and the Bullies

Dealing with anger

Bullies turn their anger outward and attack. Victims turn their anger towards themselves or family. Both need help to manage anger. Ask pupils to think of reasons and justifications for anger. Some suggestions follow. Add to the list.

 Why do people get angry?
- Because they are hurt and afraid to show it
- Because they feel frightened or inadequate or frustrated

 When is anger OK?
- If something is unfair
- If someone is being bullied

 When is anger not OK?
- If it is used unfairly or to hurt an innocent person
- If it is used to gain power over someone

Expressing anger

When working with pupils who are angry, help them learn to express it more rationally. Ask them to state the reasons for their anger calmly and to be specific: *'I'm angry because you didn't meet me at the cinema like you promised'*.

Ask them to state what they would like to happen to remedy the situation: *'You owe me an apology'* or, *'I expect you to replace the toy you broke'*.

Suggest they learn to listen to what the other person says without interrupting.

Explain that they should stick to the current problem and not bring up all the sins of the past, such as, *'You're always doing that'*.

Help them not to use blame. It is better to say, *'It makes me angry when you take my video game without asking,'* instead of, *'You're a terrible person and I hate you'*.

Indirect anger

Ask pupils to compile a list of the ways people express anger indirectly, eg:

Using drugs or alcohol

Over-eating

Starving themselves (Anorexia)

Deliberately failing

Falling ill

Becoming depressed

Who is usually hurt when anger comes out indirectly? How would they advise someone who was exhibiting signs of indirect anger? Ask them to write or dramatise a story about someone who is angry in which they include a better way to deal with it.

'I feel angry'

Ask pupils to fill in and discuss:

I feel angry when ....

I wish I could say to someone I feel angry with ....

There are times when I feel like ....

Anger is good when ....

Anger is bad when ....

I wish that .... would not be angry with me

If I tell someone I am angry, they will ....

The way I express my anger is ....

When I get angry I ....

Three positive ways to deal with my anger are ....

Use this with children privately to discuss how to deal with their feelings.

ZAP

ZAP assertiveness courses were developed by Kidscape to help children who have been severely bullied regain their self-confidence, deal with anger and frustration, and learn ways to stop being bullied. The day-long courses, which are free, usually have ten children and two teachers or trainers as facilitators. Parents of the children meet separately to learn how to help their children and their families.

80% of the children taking ZAP report that the bullying has stopped and 100% enjoy the course. ZAP, with teaching notes, is available on video or DVD for a small charge and is being replicated in schools throughout the UK. Some of the techniques used are in this book. Bullies could also benefit from a course based on ZAP. Details are on www.kidscape.org.uk

One girl wrote: *'I'm not afraid or angry anymore and I just ignore the bully. When she bullies other kids I stand up for them. I even have some friends. Thanks for ZAP.'*

About yourself questionnaire

Devise a questionnaire which encourages children and young people to think about and discuss positive attributes to help them develop a better self-image. Here are some suggestions to which you can add more of your own.

You feel angry when ....

What are your favourite television programmes? ....

What are your favourite sports, music, hobbies, activities? ....

Name five good things about yourself ....

List five words that best describe you ....

What do you like to do most? ....

What do you like to do least? ....

What is it about friends that you most value? ....

What is it that makes people like you? ....

List five things you would like to do by the time you are 21 ....

How would you change school if you had a magic wand? ....

How would you change yourself if you had a magic wand? ....

All about me

To help students learn about each other or to help you get to know a child.

1. What have you done that makes you most proud/happy?
2. Do you like your name? Would you change it? To what?
3. What is the best thing that has ever happened to you?
4. What is the weirdest/silliest thing that has ever happened to you?
5. What is the funniest thing that ever happened to you?
6. What is the saddest thing that ever happened to you?
7. Who do you most admire? Why?
8. What qualities do you look for in a friend?
9. What is your best quality?
10. What is the most important thing in your life?
11. Who is the most important person in your life?
12. What one thing would you change about yourself/your family?
13. What one thing would you change about this school?

Changing the way you communicate

Bullies and victims get set in their patterns of communication. One way to help them change is to give them specific suggestions that they can practise.

Lisa has been a victim of bullying for several months. She has taken the bullying to heart and now sees herself as a victim. When she talks to people, she hangs her head and is quite hesitant. She starts her sentences with, *'I'm sorry…'*

Gaby, on the other hand, has got away with bullying other children for years. When she wants something, she begins with, *'You, come here'* or, *'I want you to…'*

Both of these girls need to learn more positive and effective ways of communicating so they can begin to change their behaviour. The following two pages have ideas Gaby and Lisa could try and that can be used by all. Ask pupils to come up with more ideas.

Steps to take

1. Get the attention of the other person in a good way – not by interrupting, or by being nasty, or by apologising for living.
2. Look at the person you are talking to.
3. Talk confidently – not too loud and demanding or too soft and self-effacing.
4. Be efficient with your words – don't use twenty when ten will do.
5. Make your request clearly and pleasantly.

These basic communication skills can help victims to avoid getting sucked into the bully's game. They can also be used by the bully to try to get positive attention.

Effective communication

This exercise is especially good for both victims and bullies. It is a confidence builder and needs either two people or one person with a mirror.

1. Face the other person (or the mirror)

2. Think a pleasant thought and relax your face. Smile, if you can

3. Make eye contact, but don't stare – this is not a power contest.

4. State your question or request in a firm, friendly voice – don't shout or whisper

5. Don't beg, plead or demand – say clearly what you mean:
   - *'Would you please help me with my maths? I don't understand this'*
   - *'Would you like go to the cinema this Saturday?'*
   - *'Go away and leave me alone'*

6. End the conversation when you are ready:
   - *'Got to get to class. See you'*
   - *'You've been a big help. Thanks. 'Bye'*
   - *'We'll just have to agree to disagree'*

'I am proud that ...'

To help bullies and victims express pride about something they have done.

I am proud that ...

I tried very hard to

I did well in

I did not

I am good at

I helped

I always

I have improved at

I will become

My greatest achievement is

My most exciting ambition is to

Design a flag or coat of arms using some of your 'proud' statements.
Make an 'I am proud' collage with pictures or your own drawings.

Put downs

Ask all pupils to think of all the 'put down' comments people make. Write them on the board or flipchart and discuss how they make people feel. Some examples:

Go back where you came from

You're stupid

Why did you do it that way?

Get that shirt from Oxfam?

Too bad about the face

That's gay

Like your hair – NOT

Look who's escaped from the zoo

Also ask them to think of gestures or facial expressions that are 'put downs' such as:

• Holding your nose • Making monkey-like gestures and noises • Rolling your eyes

Ask pupils to spend some time observing and listing comments, gestures and facial expression that are 'put downs'. Discuss how often we use these expressions and then compile a 'build up' rather than a 'put down' list, eg: *That was a good try, well done, never mind,* etc.

Plan of action

Children caught up in bullying benefit from working out how to take control of themselves and to think about where they are going. It might be done in steps:

1. **Learn about yourself**. Am I happy with the way things are going? If not, what can I do to change things?
2. **I'm responsible**. If I am doing something to make myself or others unhappy, then it is my responsibility to change.
3. **What can I do?** What will happen if I continue on this path? What choices do I have? Make a list. What one thing can I work on today/this week?
4. **Plan it out**. What will I do/say when I see the person I am bullying or what will I do/say if I see the person who is bullying me? How will I change this relationship? Write it down, step by step.
5. **Evaluate**. What else could you have done? Did what you do help the situation or make it worse? What will you try next? Use the following exercise, 'A Good Week', to help you evaluate.

A good week

For pupils who are trying to overcome a victim mentality or bullying others (or a combination of both) this is a way to self-evaluate progress.

1. What is the nicest thing that happened to you this week? ....

2. What was the worst thing that happened? ....

3. What was the best thing you did for (or said to) someone? ....

4. What was the best thing you did for yourself? ....

5. Name one thing you changed ....

6. What did you learn about yourself? ....

7. How could this week have been improved? ....

8. My goal for next week is ....

Learn what you live

Give pupils a copy of this poem to discuss. Then follow up with the activity on page 103.

Children Learn What They Live *by Dorothy Law Nolte*
(author approved shortened version)

If children live with criticism, they learn to condemn.
If children live with hostility, they learn to fight.
If children live with ridicule, they learn to be shy.
If children live with shame, they learn to feel guilty.
If children live with encouragement, they learn confidence.
If children live with tolerance, they learn patience.
If children live with praise, they learn appreciation.
If children live with acceptance, they learn to love.
If children live with approval, they learn to like themselves.
If children live with honesty, they learn truthfulness.
If children live with security, they learn to have faith in themselves and in those about them.
If children live with friendliness, they learn that the world is a nice place in which to live.

Adapted from the book *Children Learn What They Live* ©1998 by Dorothy Law Nolte and Rachel Harris
The poem 'Children Learn What They Live' on page vi ©1972 by Dorothy Law Nolte
Used by permission of Workman Publishing Co., New York. All Rights Reserved

What bullying teaches

The poem on the previous page and this activity can lead to insightful group discussion, or personal intervention with one pupil to help them understand the harm of bullying.

Bullying teaches us:

If a child is bullied at home, he/she learns

If a child is bullied by other children, he/she learns

If a child is labelled as a bully, he/she learns

If a child bullies others, he/she learns

If a child asks for help and no one does anything, he/she learns

If a child is told he/she is stupid, he/she learns

If a child is not stopped from bullying, he/she learns

If a child tells about bullying and it gets worse, he/she learns

If a child has a teacher who is a bully, he/she learns

If bullying goes on and other children see it, they learn

If bullying is not stopped, we all learn

Making friends

Although we ask children to become friends, we seldom help them to think of how to go about it. Bullying is sometimes the result of misguided attempts by children to become part of a group or to approach someone to become a friend. Ask pupils working in small groups to discuss ways to make friends and come up with a list of ten ideas. The suggestions here were compiled by a group of 13 year olds:

- Show an interest in what people do
- Be complimentary without going overboard
- Have a pleasant expression on your face
- Offer to help
- Be welcoming to new students
- Bring something interesting to do
- Be fair

- Laugh at people's jokes
- Be kind
- Ask to join in
- Invite people to do activities
- Be willing to share
- Be amusing/tell jokes
- Organise games or activities

Ways NOT to make friends

Using the same method, ask pupils to think about behaviour that is likely to STOP them from making friends. One group thought of the following:

- Being bossy and sarcastic
- Telling others they are doing things wrong
- Talking about yourself all the time
- Talking about other students behind their backs
- Being too intense or serious all the time
- Bullying
- Bragging
- Being negative
- Lying or cheating
- Moaning all the time

Write a paper about an imaginary new student trying to make friends in your school. What obstacles might she encounter? How could you help?

Who can I turn to?

To help children think about who they would turn to for help.

Start with a circle in the middle of the page in which the child writes SELF. Then draw as many 'legs' off the circle as possible. Ask the child to label each leg with the name of a person or organisation from whom they can get help and support or comfort (eg mum, dad, gran, ChildLine, doctor, police, teachers, religious leaders, siblings, dog, neighbour, uncle, Samaritans, Kidscape, etc).

The activities in this chapter were designed mainly for bullies and victims. The next chapter is a smorgasbord for all pupils, with ideas for setting up peer support schemes and teaching positive assertiveness skills and activities to reinforce your anti-bullying ethos.

Suggestions for Everyone

Peer support schemes

The activities in this section have been road tested by teachers of primary, secondary and special needs pupils. You will know best which ones are suited to the children you teach.

'Peer support' is an umbrella term for support schemes giving pupils a chance to share concerns and explore their own solutions. They build on students' natural willingness to seek out their peers when they are experiencing problems, and on their ability to act in a genuine, empathic way toward one another.

Peer support can have a positive influence on the emotional climate of a school. Creating a framework in which pupils can support each other recognises the vital role they can play in making positive changes in their own lives and those of their peers. These schemes can dramatically reduce bullying.

Peer support options

The model chosen should be clearly defined, and the role and responsibilities should be understood and supported by the whole school community.

Peer listeners provide a confidential service as active listeners and facilitators, offering a safe place for pupils to share their concerns and to explore solutions.

Peer mediators trained in conflict resolution strategies may act as intermediaries in response to bullying situations.

Peer mentors are often given a specific focus, such as acting as a befriender to pupils in a new school or as a support for pupils who are vulnerable.

Whichever approach you adopt, it should be compatible with policies and procedures that address issues such as anti-bullying, child protection, confidentiality, record-keeping and equal opportunities.

Peer support – a whole school approach

Peer supporters will require ongoing help and supervision and need active commitment from more than one member of staff.

- Set clear criteria for selecting those who are to be peer supporters

- Peer supporters should receive appropriate and ongoing training. Links with other schools using the same model have proved useful

- Peer support schemes should be monitored and evaluated regularly to ensure that objectives are being met and the pupils feel supported

- Issues such as establishing a rolling training programme, securing space, and allowing time for key staff to liaise with local and national support agencies should also be considered

Steps to peer support

1. Decide which kind of peer support scheme suits you and your school.
2. Decide which staff members, including a coordinator, will be responsible.
3. Research possible training courses and resources.
4. Decide your criteria for the peer supporters – age, background, personality.
5. Interview and recruit potential peer supporters.
6. Either bring in a training course or, if you feel confident, run it yourself.
7. Start with a small (one year group) peer support team and monitor carefully.
8. Evaluate and roll the programme out, if you are ready.
9. Continuously monitor and liaise with other schools.
10. Have your peer supporters try the exercises and ideas in this book.

Teaching assertiveness skills

Chronic victims and timid or shy children may have poor social skills and might not know how to ask for what they want. Aggressive or boisterous children may just take what they want, or might ask roughly or aggressively. Those in between can always use a top-up on positive ways to behave – can't we all?

It is, therefore, a good idea to do some assertiveness training exercises with the whole class. Assertiveness training teaches all children acceptable ways of behaving. If you are wondering where you will get the time to do this, perhaps you can enlist the help of a parent to help during break time or after school, if necessary.

Making a request

1. **Be clear about what you want**
2. **Make your request short,** eg *'That is my pencil. Give it back please'.*
3. **Plan and practise** even if you just go over the request in your own mind. You have to decide what you are going to say and then stick to it.

Ask pupils to work in pairs. You may wish to give them a list of requests to practise or have them make up their own. Ask pupils to take turns making a simple, assertive request, such as:

'I don't want to walk home that way – let's go a different way.'
'I will not give you my homework to copy.'
'I would like you to move, please.'
'I am listening to that music – please don't change it.'
'That is my book – please give it to me.'
'Please return my jacket now.'
'I don't want to loan you my watch.'

Responding to demands

When a bully makes a demand, it is often difficult for children and young people to know what to say. Try practising responses. Ask the children to divide into pairs, one member to play the bully and the other the victim (switching roles frequently). Encourage them to come up with creative responses, but not inflammatory ones:

'Got any sweets on you?'
'Yes, but they're horrible. My dog licked them.'

'Lend us your homework.'
'OK, but the teacher has already seen it this morning.'

'Lend us dinner money.'
'No borrowing – why not get it from the secretary?'

'We'll be waiting for you after school.'
'OK, let's arrange it with the teacher.'

'You've got my book in your bag – let me have it.'
'Your book is not in my bag.'

Saying no

If you are asked to do something that is wrong or makes you uncomfortable, say no. Be kind but firm. Don't get side-tracked into apologising for your decision or justifying it. Don't make excuses. Keep your body assertive, keep good eye-contact and don't giggle.

Work in pairs (pupils or teachers) and try the following or make up your own:

'No, I don't want to leave right now. But you can go – I'll catch up later.'
'No, I don't like that.'
'No, there is no way I can do that.'
'No, leave me alone, please. I don't want to do that now.'
'No, it is my book and I need it. Maybe I can help you find one.'
'No, it just isn't possible for me to go with you. I have too much work to do.'
'No, you cannot have my chocolate – anyway it fell on the floor.'
'No, I cannot lend you any money. I've only got enough for the bus.'

Shouting no

Teach pupils to shout 'NO' as loudly as they can if they are in trouble or danger. The shout should come from the stomach and sound like a fog horn. Practise with the students (and among staff, it's invigorating). Can be used on difficult colleagues...

Say, '*At the count of three I want you to shout No – One, two, three NOOOOOO!*' Good way to wake up a class (and your neighbours – better let them know if this is going to happen). Practise until it becomes an automatic response to danger. I used it when someone tried to mug me and it startled him, allowing me to escape.

Broken record/CD

In this exercise, practise saying the same thing over and over again like a broken record. This can be used if someone is trying to get round you or not listening. Ask the children to divide into pairs – one child to be 'A' and the other to be 'B'.

A has a new bicycle. B wants to borrow it. A doesn't want anyone to play with the new bike. B keeps trying to get the bike from A. Give the children a minute in which B keeps asking for the bike, and A keeps saying, *'No'*. B can try hard to convince A.

At the end of a minute, ask if any of the Bs got the bike? What reasons were given for wanting to borrow the bike? Was it hard for the As to keep saying no?

Repeat the exercise, but this time have A try to borrow B's new football or mobile.

Fogging

If we respond to insults with more insults, it builds up. Instead we can 'fog'. Fogging swallows up insults like a great fog-bank swallows sights and sounds. You respond to insults by saying nothing or by making a short, bland comment: *'Really?'*; *'It could be'*; *'perhaps you're right'*.

This exercise can be done either working in pairs or in a circle. If you work in a circle, you can control the exercise by letting the children or young people send 'insults' to you while you 'fog' them. Make sure that the ground rules are clear – this isn't a contest about who can come up with the most horrible insult.

If working in pairs, suggest that each pair has something impersonal to insult, such as a pencil or a book:

'That is a dumb book.'   *'That book is written by an idiot.'*
'That is such an ugly pencil.'   *'That pencil is an insult to the human race.'*

Relaxation and posture

Children can find it very hard to relax, and it is a good idea to teach them the following simple exercise. (Actually this exercise is brilliant for exhausted teachers as well, but it can lead to refusal to return to work!)

Ask the child to lie on the floor and to tense every muscle until they feel really rigid. Then ask the child slowly to relax their muscles, starting with their toes and gradually working up to their head. They should end up floppy like a rag doll.

When you are finished with relaxation, ask pupils to stand and think tall. Many children, especially those involved in bullying, have poor posture and tend to creep about. They need to learn how to stand up straight, how to walk confidently, how to make and keep eye-contact. Get them to practise in front of a mirror.

Everyone is valuable

This should be a fun, rewarding activity. The aim is for pupils to say good things about one another and to see good things about themselves. The rule is: anything written must be positive.

Each person puts their own name at the top of a piece of paper. The papers are then passed on and at each subsequent person a brief comment is added, highlighting the value of the person whose name is at the top. Everyone gets back their own piece of paper with compliments on it. Alternatively, you can tape paper to everyone's back and write comments on that, which works if pupils feel comfortable with being touched on their backs.

Needless to say, there is no deliberate attempt to know who said what about whom. (Children on Kidscape's ZAP assertiveness courses (see page 92) love this exercise and keep their papers to reread – good for egos.)

Balloon debate

This simple and popular game is known as a balloon debate. It highlights the value of individuals. Several people adopt characters, people they know a little about (historical figures, current world figures, or representatives from sport, entertainment, their religion, etc.) and the remainder of the group act as audience.

There follows a brief debate set up by whoever is in the chair. These people are in a hot-air balloon but the balloon is losing height and will crash. Only one of them (or two, or three, or however many suits the circumstances) can stay; the others must be jettisoned overboard. They each make a case for themselves to be saved, citing their value to society, contribution to history or whatever. They do not rubbish other travellers, simply make their own case. When each has stated their case, the audience is asked to vote and the person generating most votes is the one who remains on board! Remind voters they are voting for the character, not the person.

Cornucopia

To give us beleaguered teachers some quick ideas to use in a pinch:

- **Body outline** – For younger children. Ask them to lie down on a large piece of paper (rolls of heavy lining paper from a DIY shop are quite cheap) and trace an outline of their bodies. Ask the children to cut out their outline and colour it in. Use Post-it® notes on which to write about each child and attach it to the outline. Change the message as often as possible – the children will be delighted

- **Perfect school** – Ask pupils to design a perfect school in which everyone is happy and there is no bullying. (The opposite of the exercise on page 35)

- **Millionaire** – Tell pupils they have each inherited £1,000,000, of which they must use 90% to eradicate bullying.   After they have stopped all bullying, they can then use the remaining 10% of the money for themselves and must use that 10% to make their own lives happier. What will they do?

Cornucopia

- **Bully gang** – Ask pupils to write a story about a young person who finds that he/she is being pulled into a bully gang and being pressured to start bullying a person they have been friends with in the past. Ask them to write about what the character might be thinking and feeling and how he/she resolves the problem. Use as a springboard to discuss resisting peer pressure

- **Victim viewpoint** – After the students have completed the exercise above, ask them to write the same story from the viewpoint of the victim. He/she will be confused, frightened and worried, especially when one of her/his friends joins in the gang bullying

Cornucopia

- **Bulletin board** – Ask older pupils to look for references to bullying, including racist attacks or attacks on gay or lesbian people or incidents of suicide or suicide attempts attributed to bullying in the press. Use these stories to create a bulletin board and to discuss bullying

- **Mural** – Ask younger children to co-operate on drawing and decorating a class mural. On one panel draw a playground where bullying is happening and on another panel a playground where everyone is having a good time and where there is no bullying. Discuss your own playground and think of ways that could make it like the 'no bullying' panel

That's all the pages the publishers would let me have, but I hope I have given you a taste of how to tackle bullying. You must be the kind of teacher we all want for our children because you were interested enough to read this book and to try to stop bullying in your school. As a fellow teacher, I thank you for that. You probably have great ideas and have tried other techniques that work. I really would like to hear from you: michele@kidscape.org.uk

Websites

The following organisations have a good selection of current resources and links to lots of other useful groups:

Kidscape	**www.kidscape.org.uk**
Andrea Adams Trust (Workplace Bullying)	**www.andreaadamstrust.org**
Anti-Bullying Alliance	**www.ncb.org.uk/aba**
Anti-Bullying Network Scotland	**www.antibullying.net**
BBC	**www.bbc.co.uk/schools/communities/ onionstreet/advice/bullying.shtml**
Beat Bullying	**www.bbclic.com**
Bullying Online	**www.bullying.co.uk**
Childnet	**www.kidsmart.org.uk**
Circle Time	**www.circle-time.co.uk**
Department for Education & Skills	**www.dfes.gov.uk/bullying**
Joint Action Against Homophobic Bullying	**www.intercomtrust.org.uk**
The Mental Health Foundation	**www.mentalhealth.org.uk**
Stonewall (Homophobic Bullying)	**www.stonewall.org.uk**

Books and other resources

Other books about bullying by Michele Elliott. (Available from Kidscape, 2 Grosvenor Gardens, London SW1W 0DH, or download information from the website on page 125)

How to Stop Bullying: A Kidscape Training Guide
Bullying: A Practical Guide to Coping for Schools
Bully Free Activities for 15-20 year olds
Bully Wise Guide For 10-16 year olds
Beat The Bullies – Willow Street Kids For 7-11 year olds
101 Ways to Deal with Bullying: A Guide for Parents

Kidscape Video/DVD
Bully Free – based on ZAP Assertiveness Courses for 9-16 year olds

Leaflets:
Preventing Racist Bullying
Stop Bullying
You Can Beat Bullying
Preventing Bullying

About the author

Michele Elliott

Michele is a teacher, psychologist with 35 years' experience, and the founder director of the children's charity KIDSCAPE. She is considered to be the UK's foremost expert on prevention of bullying, having pioneered the first research and books on the subject in 1984. Since then she has written 23 books on subjects including bullying, abuse and parenting. She regularly contributes articles and comments to national newspapers, radio and television, as well as to professional journals.

Michele works with the Home Office, the Department for Education and Skills, the Department of Health, the World Health Organisation, charities and other agencies, and consults with numerous committees and enquiries. She is a Winston Churchill Fellow.

Married to a 30 years+ veteran teacher of 13 year olds and the mother of two sons, Michele describes herself as a 'demented, elderly mother and teacher'. Contact her on michele@kidscape.org.uk.

Order Form

Your details

Name _____

Position _____

School _____

Address _____

_____

_____

Telephone _____

Fax _____

E-mail _____

VAT No. (EC only) _____

Your Order Ref _____

Please send me:

No. copies

Stop Bullying _____ Pocketbook ☐

_____ Pocketbook ☐

_____ Pocketbook ☐

_____ Pocketbook ☐

_____ Pocketbook ☐

Order by Post

**Teachers'
Pocketbooks**
Laurel House, Station Approach
Alresford, Hants. SO24 9JH UK

Order by Phone, Fax or Internet

Telephone: +44 (0)1962 735573
Facsimile: +44 (0)1962 733637
E-mail: sales@teacherspocketbooks.co.uk
Web: www.teacherspocketbooks.co.uk